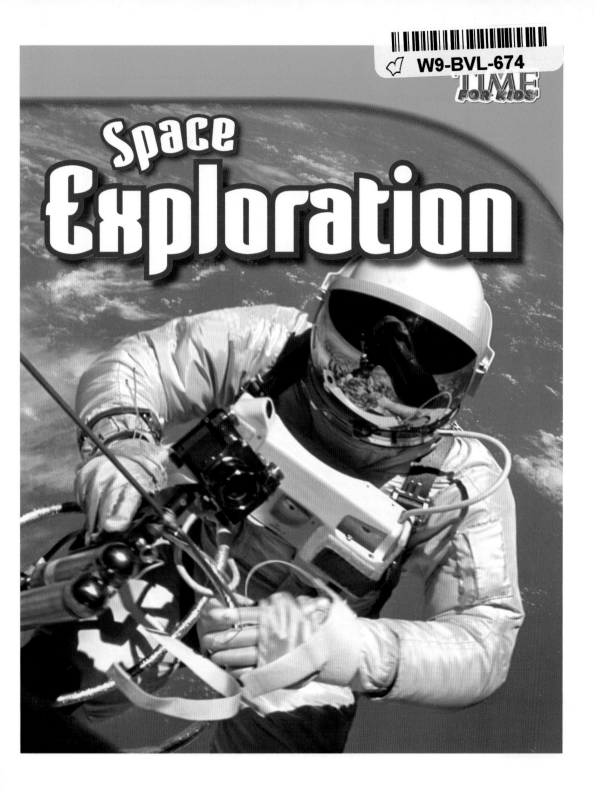

Space Exploration

TIME FOR KIDS

Christine Dugan

Consultant

Timothy Rasinski, Ph.D.
Kent State University
Mark Sisson, Engineer

Publishing Credits

Dona Herweck Rice, *Editor-in-Chief*
Robin Erickson, *Production Director*
Lee Aucoin, *Creative Director*
Conni Medina, M.A.Ed., *Editorial Director*
Jamey Acosta, *Editor*
Heidi Kellenberger, *Editor*
Lexa Hoang, *Designer*
Lesley Palmer, *Designer*
Stephanie Reid, *Photo Editor*
Rachelle Cracchiolo, M.S.Ed., *Publisher*

Based on writing from *TIME For Kids*.

TIME For Kids and the *TIME For Kids* logo are registered trademarks of TIME Inc.
Used under license.

Teacher Created Materials

5301 Oceanus Drive
Huntington Beach, CA 92649-1030
http://www.tcmpub.com
ISBN 978-1-4333-3674-4
© 2012 Teacher Created Materials, Inc.
Printed in Malaysia
Thumbprints.27318

Table of Contents

A New World

In 1492, the explorer Christopher Columbus discovered a "New World." The truth is the world had always been there, but it was new to Columbus and his people.

More than 450 years later, most of our planet had been "discovered." But people still wanted to explore, just as Columbus did. So, where else was there to go? Up! People began to explore space.

▲ Christopher Columbus traveled by ship across the ocean.

Space is a vast, seemingly endless area for people to explore. We have learned much about space over the last few **decades**. But luckily for today's explorers, we still have much more to discover!

Today's explorers use different kinds of ships, but they have the same sense of adventure. ▶

Early Exploration

Modern space exploration officially began on October 4, 1957. That is when the first man-made **satellite** was launched into space. It was called Sputnik 1, and it was built by the **Soviet Union**. It successfully **orbited** Earth for six months.

On November 3, 1957, the Soviet Union sent Sputnik 2 into space. This time there was a passenger—a dog named Laika. She lived for several days. Sadly, Laika died of **heat exhaustion** caused by rising temperatures in the satellite.

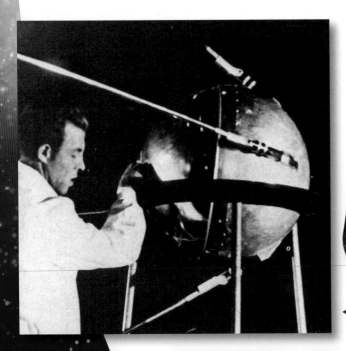

◀ Sputnik 1

The Soviet Union

The Union of Soviet Socialist Republics (USSR), also called the Soviet Union, was a group of united countries in Asia and Europe. Russia was the largest country in the union. In 1991, the Soviet Union divided into individual countries.

What Is It?

A man-made satellite is an object people place into space to circle Earth, other planets, or the sun.

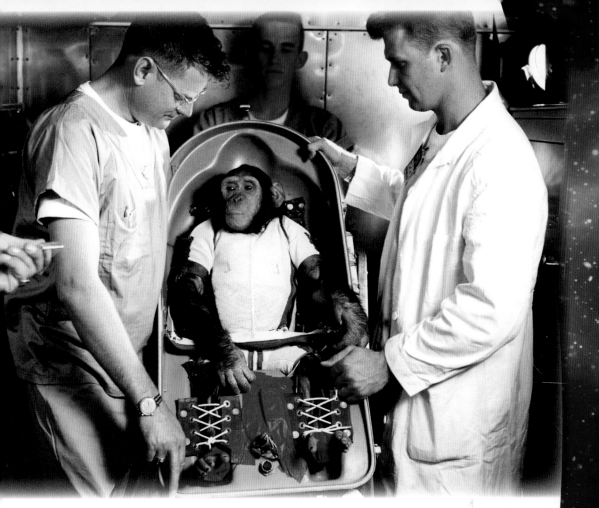

▲ Ham, a chimpanzee, went into space in 1961.

Two more dogs were sent into space, but they returned home safely by parachute. Next a chimpanzee named Ham went up. He returned to Earth in perfect health. Four months after Sputnik 1 was launched, the United States sent Explorer 1 to orbit Earth.

In addition to dogs and monkeys, people have sent frogs, mice, fish, bees, flies, ants, sea urchins, and more than 2,000 jellyfish into space! Scientists study these animals to learn about the effects of space on living things.

NASA

People had finally found a way to reach space. Now they hoped to find a way to send humans there. So, in 1958, the United States founded the **National Aeronautics** (air-uh-NAW-tiks) **and Space Administration**, also called **NASA**. Aeronautics is the study, design, and building of aircraft. NASA organized space travel for the United States.

▼ the first US astronauts

In 1961, US President John F. Kennedy offered a challenge. He asked the nation to land a person on the moon by the end of the decade.

What Does NASA Do?

Scientists and engineers at NASA research space and everything about it. They also help astronauts when they go into space.

▲ President Kennedy was an important supporter of space exploration.

◀ Astronaut Alan Shepard was the first American in space.

Project Mercury was the first **manned** US mission in space. NASA wanted a spacecraft to orbit Earth. They also wanted to learn how people could travel and live in space. Starting in 1961, **astronauts** made six trips into space during Project Mercury. Now, people were true space travelers!

Project Gemini came next. There were 12 Gemini flights between 1965 and 1966. During the flights, NASA learned more about what could happen on a longer trip in space.

◀ *Gemini*

Race to Space

Yuri Gagarin, a cosmonaut from the Soviet Union, was the first human to fly into space. Aboard the *Vostok 1*, he orbited Earth one time on April 12, 1961. Today, a crater on the moon is named after him.

▲ Yuri Gagarin

◄ Rockets were used to launch astronauts into space. They were slowly raised to an upright position for takeoff.

Finally, NASA was ready for Project Apollo, the mission that would send people to the moon. It was a thrilling idea for people on Earth. On July 20, 1969, astronauts landed and walked on the moon for the first time. People were amazed when astronaut Neil Armstrong stepped onto the moon and said, "That's one small step for man, one giant leap for mankind."

▼ When the *Apollo 11* astronauts landed on the moon, President Kennedy's challenge was met.

How Much?

Space travel isn't cheap! In 1973 the total cost of the Apollo Project was $25 billion dollars. Today that's $125 billion dollars!

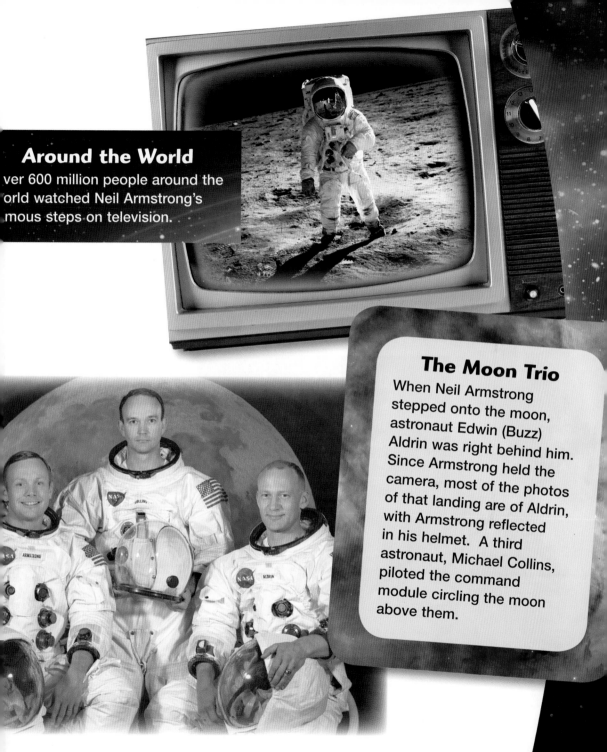

Around the World

Over 600 million people around the world watched Neil Armstrong's famous steps on television.

The Moon Trio

When Neil Armstrong stepped onto the moon, astronaut Edwin (Buzz) Aldrin was right behind him. Since Armstrong held the camera, most of the photos of that landing are of Aldrin, with Armstrong reflected in his helmet. A third astronaut, Michael Collins, piloted the command module circling the moon above them.

During the Apollo missions, astronauts also did experiments in space. The 11 Apollo trips from 1968 to 1972 were some of the most amazing moments in space history.

Space Shuttles

In 1972, NASA decided to look at space travel a little differently. Until then, astronauts traveled into space in rockets used only once. NASA started to think about building a **space shuttle** that could be used again and again. They wanted something that could take off like a rocket, but land like an airplane. After many years of building and testing, the *Columbia* space shuttle went into space in 1981. It was a success!

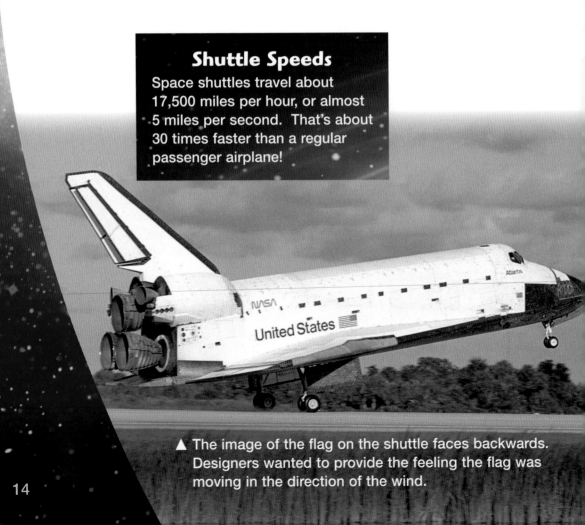

Shuttle Speeds

Space shuttles travel about 17,500 miles per hour, or almost 5 miles per second. That's about 30 times faster than a regular passenger airplane!

▲ The image of the flag on the shuttle faces backwards. Designers wanted to provide the feeling the flag was moving in the direction of the wind.

rocket

crew compartment

shuttle

fuselage

payload bay doors

wing

stabilizer

Shuttle Sign Off

In 2011, the last space shuttle landed at NASA's Kennedy Space Center. The space shuttle program was over. NASA workers gathered to celebrate the work they had done. People all around the world are working to develop new ways of traveling into space.

Space Tragedies

Space travel may seem common today, but it is still dangerous. Sadly, sometimes there are accidents, and astronauts are injured or killed while on a mission.

On January 27, 1967, the three astronauts aboard *Apollo 1* were killed on the launchpad during a test before takeoff. A fire started in the **cockpit** and they were unable to escape.

A Near Miss

In 1970, due to an explosion, the astronauts aboard *Apollo 13* were unable to land on the moon and almost didn't make it back to Earth. Because of their skills, and with the help of the team at NASA, they avoided tragedy and came home heroes.

In 1986, on its tenth mission, the space shuttle *Challenger* exploded in air just 73 seconds after takeoff. All seven crew members were killed.

A second shuttle disaster happened on February 1, 2003. The *Columbia*, NASA's oldest space shuttle, was lost just 16 minutes before it was supposed to land. This was its 28th flight. Again, all crew members died.

This image was taken by a satellite. It shows the *Challenger* above Earth's clouds, with its bay doors open.

Hubble Telescope

Have you ever seen a picture of another planet? Did you wonder how someone took that picture? Well, maybe it wasn't a person. It might have been taken by the **Hubble Telescope**.

The Hubble Telescope is a very special tool. It travels in space. While there, it takes pictures of stars, planets, and other objects. It has been in space since 1990.

The Hubble Telescope allows us to explore space in a new way. We can learn about objects that are so far away we couldn't possibly travel to them right now.

◀ Hubble Telescope

a photograph of a galaxy taken by NA Hubble Telescope ▼

Edwin Hubble
The Hubble Telescope was named after Edwin Hubble, a famous astronomer.

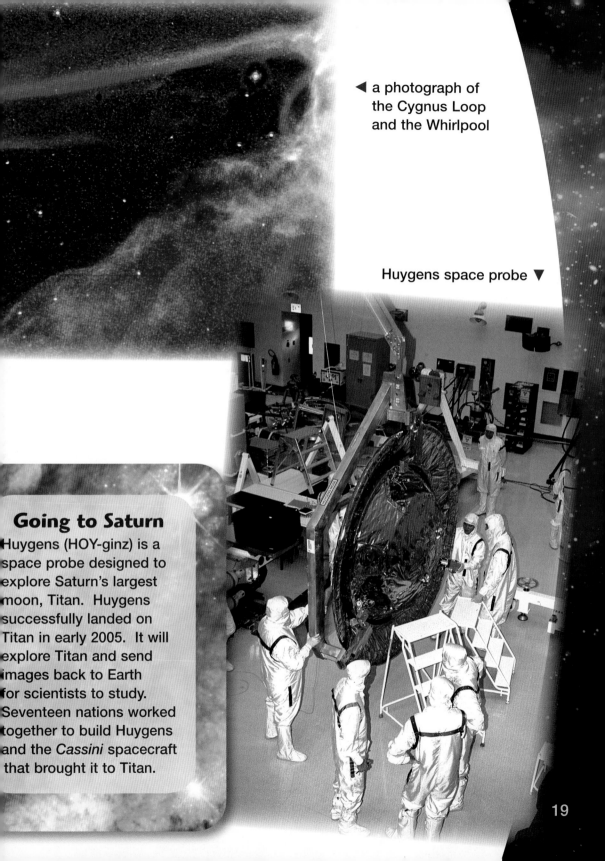

◄ a photograph of the Cygnus Loop and the Whirlpool

Huygens space probe ▼

Going to Saturn

Huygens (HOY-ginz) is a space probe designed to explore Saturn's largest moon, Titan. Huygens successfully landed on Titan in early 2005. It will explore Titan and send images back to Earth for scientists to study. Seventeen nations worked together to build Huygens and the *Cassini* spacecraft that brought it to Titan.

International Space Station

Today, one of the most exciting things in space is the **International Space Station**. It is the largest object in space made by people. It is like a small city in space.

The first crew began living on the space station in 2000. Astronauts from 16 countries work together there. Each country hopes to learn more about space. This space city is already big, but it is still growing. When it is finished, it will be a little longer than a football field.

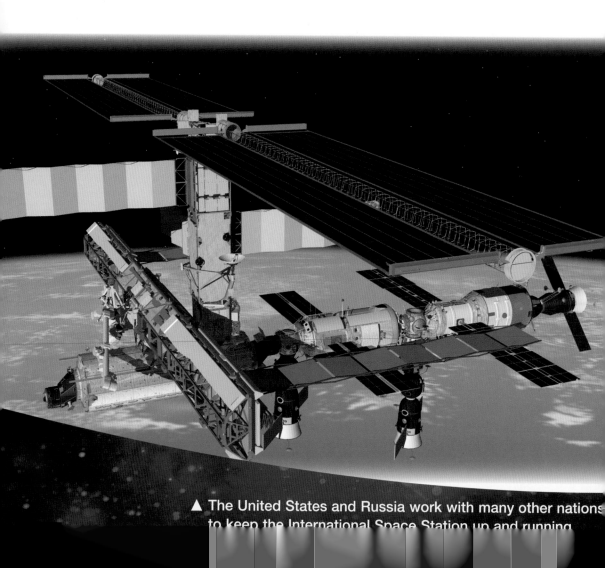

▲ The United States and Russia work with many other nations to keep the International Space Station up and running.

▲ The Mir space station

Space Station History

The International Space Station is not the first of its kind. Here are some important moments in space station history.

Salyut 1

● The first proposal for a manned station was in the United States in 1869, in a science fiction book.

● The Soviet Union launched the first space station, Salyut 1, in 1971. The first crew arrived days later but could not get the hatch open and left.

Skylab

● The second Soviet crew arrived at Salyut 1 and spent 22 days on board. Sadly, they died on the way home when air leaked from their capsule.

● The United States sent its first space station, Skylab, into orbit in 1973. Three crews lived on it from then until February 1974. Skylab fell to Earth five years later, killing a cow in Australia.

Mir

● In 1986, Russia launched the first module of the Mir space station. It was almost continually manned until it was brought back to Earth in March 2001. It crashed into the ocean of the South Pacific.

The International Space Station orbits Earth every 90 minutes. Sometimes you can even see the space station from Earth when it is traveling over your city.

What do the astronauts do every day? They have a lot of work. First, they must keep the space station running properly. Their lives depend on it! They also stay busy doing experiments.

▲ an astronaut tests equipment

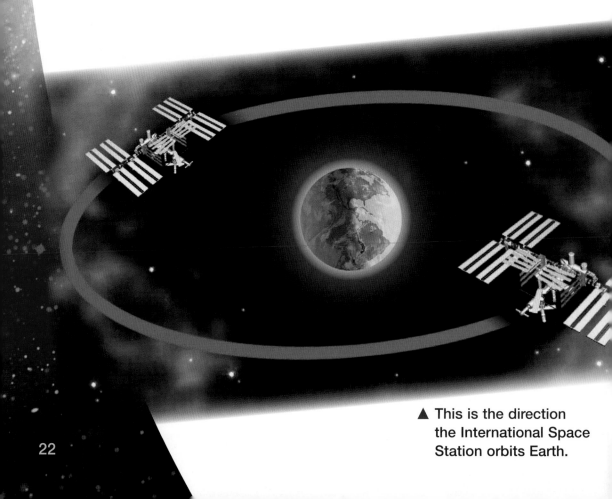

▲ This is the direction the International Space Station orbits Earth.

▲ There are some places in space where people cannot go. Some places are just too hot or too cold. Robots, such as this Mars Exploration Rover, have been designed to go to those places.

Space Inventions

Many things invented for use in space are used by people today in everyday life. Video-game joysticks were developed from technology used to control roving devices on the moon. Smoke detectors were first used in an orbiting space station to help detect poisonous gases. Does anyone you know wear invisible braces? They are made of a tough material NASA developed for spacecraft. Do some research and you will find countless other space inventions you use in your daily life.

One thing the astronauts want to learn is how weightlessness affects the body. Astronauts experiment on themselves to see how their bodies handle living in space. In this way, we learn how everyone might be able to live there safely. The experiments also teach us more about the health of people here on Earth.

◄ Astronaut Leroy Chiao floats in one of the labs in the International Space Station.

Astronaut C. Michae Foale uses a digital camera to photogra his observations in space. ▼

On the space station, astronauts also study Earth and take photographs of it. They can see things from space that we cannot see here at home.

▲ This view of Earth was taken from the International Space Station.

Our future in Space

So, we have explored space using rockets, space shuttles, and space stations. What is next? People will discover ways to spend longer periods of time in space. Scientists are studying ways to make space travel easier. In time, we will be able to explore great distances.

▲ In the fall of 2004, Burt Rutan and his team won the Ansari X-Prize for being the first private manned mission to send a reusable spaceship into space twice in two weeks.

In the future, the rockets that travel into space may be owned by people, not by NASA. On June 21, 2004, a rocket plane called *SpaceShipOne* was launched from a California desert and took a quick trip to the boundary of space. Other such trips have followed. This event means people may someday fly into space just as easily as they fly on airplanes today.

▲ *SpaceShipOne* is a revolution in civilian space travel.

LIFE

THE NEXT GIANT LEAP
A Wild Ride On
SpaceShipOne

Gretchen Wilson Kick-Starts Country • Have We Found the Perfect Town?   WEEKEND OF OCTOBER **22** 2004

Famous Astronauts

Who are the brave men and women who make space exploration possible? Here are a few of the most famous astronauts from the United States.

Alan Shepard was the pilot of the first US rocket sent into space.

John Glenn was the first US astronaut to orbit Earth. He orbited three times in about five hours. He was also the oldest man to go into space when he returned there in 1998. He was 77 years old.

Guion S. Bluford, Jr. flew on the *Challenger* in 1983. He was the first African American man in space.

Sally Ride was the first American woman to travel into space. She was aboard the *Challenger* in 1983.

Ellison Shoji Onizuka was the first Asian American in space. He flew on two space shuttle missions. He died on the *Challenger* in 1986.

Mae Jemison was the first African American woman in space. She was aboard the *Endeavor* in 1992.

With the help of NASA and brave astronauts, we learn more about space every day. Only time will tell what the future holds for space exploration.

Glossary

aeronautics—the design and construction of aircraft

astronauts—people who pilot, direct, or work on the crew of a spacecraft

cockpit—the area in a shuttle where the pilot sits

cosmonaut—an astronaut from the Soviet Union or Russia

decades—time periods of ten years

heat exhaustion—the state of being very tired or sick due to extreme heat

Hubble Telescope—a tool that takes pictures in space

International Space Station—a permanent "city" in space, on which sixteen countries work together to research space and Earth

manned—having people on board

NASA—the National Aeronautics and Space Administration, an organization that organizes space travel for the United States

orbited—moved in a circle or oval shape around an object in space

satellite—an object launched into space to orbit Earth or another body in space

Soviet Union—the Union of Soviet Socialist Republics; ending in 1991, a group of united countries in Asia and Europe, with Russia being its largest country

space shuttle—a type of spacecraft that can be used many times and takes off like a rocket, but lands like an airplane

Index

About the Author

Christine Dugan earned her B.A. from the University of California, San Diego. She taught elementary school for several years before deciding to take on a different challenge in the field of education. She has worked as a product developer, writer, editor, and sales assistant for various educational publishing companies. In recent years, Christine earned her M.A. in Education and is currently working as a freelance author and editor. She lives in the Pacific Northwest with her husband and two daughters.

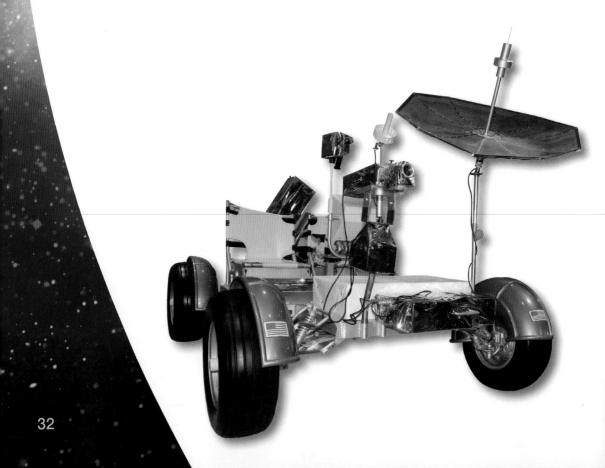